Oh Baby, The Places You Could Have Gone

Sermon preached Sunday, January 15, 2012

by Rev. Jason Biette

at

Oakwood Bible Church

Troy, New York

Rev. Jason Biette, *Oh Baby, the Places You Could Have Gone*

Copyright © 2012 Rev. Jason Biette

Cover photograph by Jessica L. Biette

Published in the United States of America

PREFACE

The following is the manuscript of a sermon which I preached at Oakwood Bible Church on January 15, 2012. The reasons for publishing this sermon are as follows...

1. I was encouraged by several people, not the least of which was my wife, to try to find a way to give this sermon a broader audience.
2. I have become convinced that this is a message for all Christians, at least in America, to hear and to act upon.
3. My heartfelt desire is to work faithfully toward the increase of God's Kingdom, and my hope is

that in some small way God may choose to use this to that end.

Publishing a sermon can be tricky business, as someone somewhere once said, "All preaching is plagiarism." This was originally written to be communicated verbally to a congregation, and the attention to detail is not nearly as rigorous as something which is written to be published.

My prayer is that my thought pattern has primarily been shaped by God's Word, but I would be remiss to not acknowledge all of the people who God has used to help shape and mold my understanding of His Word and world. I am sure that my voice, whether spoken or written, more often sounds like these people, and I can only hope that the old saying is true which states that 'imitation if the most sincere form of flattery'.

Whether or not you may be interested in looking into some of those Colonels in God's army you can always check out resources on our church website at www.oakwoodbiblechurch.com, or my blog at www.jasonbiette.wordpress.com. There you will find material which I can only assume will be as edifying to you as it was to me, but please remember, no list of this nature can ever be complete.

In addition to all the help that these teachers have been to me, no one has had a greater impact on my spiritual life than Rev. James DuJack, who has been my Pastor since I was in the fifth grade, and thankfully continues to do so. This first, rather small and humble publication of mine is dedicated to him and the life that he poured out for the congregation of Oakwood Bible Church in Troy, NY.

I have done my best to reference any sources that are pertinent to the preparation of this sermon, and therefore have added citations where I thought appropriate. This was done during the preparation of the manuscript for publication, and although it is not an afterthought, was never part of the primary work of sermon preparation.

Finally, I would like to thank all who have made this possible. First, my God who called me into a covenant relationship with himself some 34 years ago, and never let me go, continuing to make good on His promises. I would like to thank my parents for their faithful obedience to our Heavenly Father, raising my brother and me in the nurture and admonition of the Lord. I would like to thank the congregation of Oakwood Bible Church and the Elder Board for calling me into ministry, for their support and encouragement, and for the opportunity that they provide for me to study God's Word in order to preach and teach it. Lastly I would like to thank my wife for being my wife. It is a vocation not a vacation, but she does it with faith and class. She has supported me in everything that I have done; she has blessed me with a wonderful family, and she makes for a great editor. SHMILY.

CONTENTS

Oh Baby, the Places You Could Have Gone

Sermon Texts

Let us hear the word of the Lord this morning...

*O LORD, you have searched me and known me!
You know when I sit down and when I rise up; you
discern my thoughts from afar. You search out my
path and my lying down and are acquainted with all
my ways. Even before a word is on my tongue,
behold, O LORD, you know it altogether. You hem
me in, behind and before, and lay your hand upon
me. Such knowledge is too wonderful for me; it is
high; I cannot attain it. (Psalm 139:1-6)*

For you formed my inward parts; you knitted me together in my mother's womb. I praise you, for I am fearfully and wonderfully made. Wonderful are your works; my soul knows it very well. My frame was not hidden from you, when I was being made in secret, intricately woven in the depths of the earth. Your eyes saw my unformed substance; in your book were written, every one of them, the days that were formed for me, when as yet there was none of them. How precious to me are your thoughts, O God! How vast is the sum of them! If I would count them, they are more than the sand. I awake, and I am still with you. (Psalm 139:13-18)

Introduction

Next Sunday, January 22, is Sanctity of Life Sunday, a day that we as Christians should certainly mark. I had every intention of dealing with that theme from the scriptures, next week, until I found that our readings for today included the above verses from Psalm 139. So, although Sanctity of Life Sunday is one week from today, and I would encourage all of you to be meditating on God's word and praying for God's help and mercy in regard to this issue all week and next Sunday, we are going to pause for a moment to see some of what His Word has to say about this topic today.

On March 2, 1904, Theodor Geisel was born. He lived 87 years, and during the course of his life he published 46 books. Many of which have been considered to be classic works. He also worked as an illustrator, a political cartoonist, and in the animation department of the U.S. army.

He was quite a complex individual. He loved children, and loved to entertain them, although he had none of his own by either of his two wives. Politically he was a mixed bag, like so many of us. He was a lifetime liberal democrat and supporter of President Franklin D. Roosevelt and the New Deal, but he was also passionately opposed to fascism, as his political cartoons made clear.

His worldview certainly comes out in the topics he chose to write about: environmentalism and anti-consumerism, racial equality, the arms race, Hitler and anti-authoritarianism, and anti-isolationism and internationalism.[1]

Interestingly, he was also known to be a believing and practicing Christian. He belonged to a church in his hometown of Springfield, Massachusetts, he was the son of Christian parents who raised him in a Christian home, and he attended mandatory chapel services at both Dartmouth and Oxford. By any account he had a strong religious background.

---

[1] Wikipedia contributors. "Dr. Seuss." *Wikipedia, The Free Encyclopedia, 30 Apr. 2012. Web. 15 May. 2012.*

So, what is it about Mr. Geisel that we are talking about him today? I believe a famous quote from one of his works can shed some light on that.

Don't give up! I believe in you all! A person's a person, no matter how small![2]

Mr. Theodor Geisel was *the* Dr. Seuss, and that was a famous and well known line from 'Horton Hears a Who.' His wife has written…

"[he was] intrigued by research into the development of babies while they are in their mother's womb. The fact that they could hear sounds – and might actually respond to the voices of their parents- was both exciting and mystifying to him. Researchers found increased uterine activity during reading [The Cat and the Hat] – and a gradual settling down afterward. This response to the book continued after delivery. The baby apparently recalled having heard the story before …in utero![3]

Now, all of this is fine and good, but even more importantly is what the Bible has to say about this

---

[2] Seuss, Dr. *Horton Hears a Who!*. New York: Random House, 1954. 47.

[3] Rabe, Trish, comp. *Oh, Baby, the Places You'll Go! A Book to be Read in Utero.* 1st ed. New York: Random House, Inc., 1997. Web. 15 May. 2012.
<http://books.google.com/books?id=Z3PYM8CY11QC&printsec=frontcover&source=gbs_ge_summary_r&cad=0

topic, and it has a lot to say about it, starting in Psalm 139.

Even Before Birth

I want to break down the verses that we have this morning into three sections. First, verses 1 through 6 speak about God's intimate knowledge of His people. Second, verses 13 through 16 describes life in a very dark place, a place that only God's knowledge could penetrate; a mother's womb. Third, and finally, verses 17 and 18 describe how delightful it is to know of God's knowledge.

In the first section we find an affirmation that the Lord knows all there is to know about us. The Psalmist states that 'you have searched me and know me.' We recognize, along with the Psalmist, that God knows all of our activities, He knows all of our words, and He knows all of our thoughts, even our deepest thoughts. God's knowledge of us goes beyond what we could ever comprehend. It is too wonderful. It is beyond our ability, even as we read in Deuteronomy 29:29...

"The secret things belong to the Lord our God, but the things that are revealed belong to us and to our children forever, that we may do all the words of this law.(Deuteronomy 29:29)

As the Psalmist continues he illustrates the extent of this knowledge. He paints a picture in verses 11-12...

If I say, "surely the darkness shall cover me, and the light about me be night," even the darkness is not dark to you; the night is bright as the day, for darkness is as light with you. (Psalm 139:11-12)

...which he then explains in verses 13-16. That is that God saw us and loved us even before we were born.

The Psalmist moves from the generalities of verses 11 and 12 to a particular dark place where the Lord still was able to see into and care for us. God was active even when we were in our mother's womb, when we began unformed and then grew and developed, God was the One who formed us. In fact, even before our mothers knew that they were pregnant, as the Psalmist puts it "my frame was not hidden from you, when I was being made in secret," He knew us and was active in our lives. The Lord was already showing care.

Fearfully and Wonderfully Made

Verse 14 of our text describes the worshipper's marvel over the mysterious process of a growing and developing baby in the mother's womb, but it also tells us something very special about God's work in the life of His people. In the Hebrew the phrase 'wonderfully made' has a slightly unusual spelling which can allow it to be translated "I am fearfully set apart."[4] This is the term that we find used elsewhere in referring to God setting His people apart. For instance, in Exodus 8 we read…

But on that day I will set apart the land of Goshen, where my people dwell, so that no swarms of flies

[4] Dennis, Lane T., ed. *ESV Study Bible, English Standard Version.* Wheaton: Crossway Bibles, 2008. 1116-17. Print.

shall be there, that you may know that I am the Lord in the midst of the earth.(Exodus 8:22)

Another example is found in Psalm 4...

But know that the Lord has set apart the godly for himself; the Lord hears when I call to him. (Psalm 4:3)

We also see this same phrase used when a distinction is made between God's people and those who are not His people.

But the Lord will make a distinction between the livestock of Israel and the livestock of Egypt, so that nothing of all that belongs to the people of Israel shall die."(Exodus 9:4)

But not a dog shall growl against any of the people of Israel, either man or beast, that you may know that the Lord makes a distinction between Egypt and Israel.'(Exodus 11:7)

For how shall it be known that I have found favor in your sight, I and your people? Is it not in your going with us, so that we are distinct, I and your people, from every other people on the face of the earth?"(Exodus 33:16)

So it seems that the Psalmist is not only affirming that we are "fearfully and wonderfully made", and certainly we are, but that in being formed by the hand of God we are also specially set apart by Him.

The implication of this is extremely important. The faithful person singing this during the time of the Old Testament would be the child of faithful parents. It would be, and is an affirmation that God set His special love upon that individual, the worshipper, from the earliest stages of his personal life.[5]

Yet you are he who took me from the womb; you made me trust you at my mother's breasts. On you was I cast from my birth, and from my mother's womb you have been my God. (Psalm 22:9-10)

For you, o Lord, are my hope, my trust, o Lord, from my youth. Upon you I have leaned from before my birth; you are he who took me from my mother's womb. My praise is continually of you. (Psalm 71:5-6)

Finally, we see in verses 17 and 18 what our proper response is to this knowledge. Understanding God's intimate knowledge of us causes us to recognize the value, even the preciousness of his thoughts. He knows us so completely that we should value the mind of God over all other things.

---

[5] Ibid. 1117.

Personhood

Dr. Seuss wrote that "a person's a person no matter how small," and although it has been hotly contested, and stated by himself and his wife that this statement and book really had nothing to do with the issue of abortion, even today the debate still very often revolves around personhood.[6] But we have already shown that Psalm 139 speaks powerfully to the nature of unborn human life, as well as other Scriptures.

Briefly then, let us now look at the question of personhood, from the place that we should value above all other things, God's thoughts. In verse 13

---

[6] Wikipedia contributors. "Dr. Seuss." *Wikipedia, The Free Encyclopedia, 30 Apr. 2012. Web. 15 May. 2012.*

of Psalm 139 there is a celebration of God's involvement in the development of this baby. The word here that is translated 'inward parts' is the Hebrew word for kidneys. Biblically this is the seat of affections.[7]

It is the hidden part where grief may be experienced…

> *His archers surround me. He slashes open my kidneys and does not spare; he pours out my gall on the ground. (Job 16:13)*

It is where the conscience exists…

> *I bless the Lord who gives me counsel; in the night also my heart [kidneys] instructs me. (Psalm 16:7)*

It is where deep spiritual distress can be felt…

> *When my soul was embittered, when I was pricked in heart, (Psalm 73:21)*

Verse 16 makes clear that God's knowledge of the Psalmist reached even to his earliest development in the womb. Also, David confesses that he was a sinner from conception, as we read in Psalm 51…

> *Behold, I was brought forth in iniquity, and in sin did my mother conceive me. (Psalm 51:5)*

---

[7] Dennis, 2538.

Therefore, when looking at these points as a whole, God's Word makes it clear that personhood begins at conception. David attributes moral accountability to conception, just as sinfulness is connected to conception and it is only persons that can be morally accountable because they are sinners. It is only persons that can be described as possessing the seat of affections at the earliest stages of life, from conception.[8] Besides, we know, and I would submit that every one of them knows, whether they would admit it or not, that "a person's a person no matter how small."[9]

---

[8] ibid, 2539.
[9] Seuss. 47.

Statistics Speak

So, what should we, as the Church think about abortion and what should we be doing about it?

Since 1972, 40 short years, over 52 million abortions have taken place in America.

Wikipedia list 242 countries in the world, and the number 52 million is more than or equal to the population of 219 out of 242 of those countries.[10]

There are only 23 countries that have a population greater than the number of abortions that have taken

---

[10] Wikipedia contributors. "List of Countries by Population." *Wikipedia, The Free Encyclopedia.* Wikipedia, The Free Encyclopedia, 15 May. 2012. Web. 15 May. 2012.

place in this country in the last 40 years. This can be difficult to put into perspective, but it might help to see that as of October 2011 the population of Canada was 34.6 million, almost 20 million less than the number of abortions in the last 40 years in America.

Certainly this is a sin that the Church needs to continue to fight against and shine a light upon. But I think another set of statistics could be very helpful in moving us along to understanding how it is that God wants us to fight this battle, and other ones like it.

Since 1972, out of 8 Presidents 5 have been Republican, and out of 40 years about 26 have been under the leadership of a Republican President.

I am old enough to remember what it was like back in the 1980's, and how vocal the Church's opposition to abortion was. Most of us here can remember that for a long time it was considered a conservative litmus test for judging political candidates. That fire in the church's belly has certainly died down to a smoldering ember, at best. The Evangelical conservative right does not seem to make too much of a big deal about this anymore. We hear people talk about it here and there, and it comes up occasionally, but as a collective group we have moved on to being terrified about losing this country. That does not include too many discussions about abortion any more, as most of the time we are concerned with issues of economic models and personal freedoms. I want to be absolutely clear here, those are equally important and valid. It all is, but I cannot be easily convinced that God will allow this country any more mercy, regardless of who wins the next Presidential election, if we continue to go down the same sinful path that we have been going down.

A Civilized Culture?

The Roman empire was considered the paragon of civilization in its heyday, and even by historians today, but it was Cicero that wrote in the 'Twelve Tables of Roman Law' during the last century B.C. that… "deformed infants shall be killed"; and it was Plutarch during the first century A.D. who wrote that it was not uncommon for Romans to "offer up their own children, and those who had no children would buy little ones from poor people and 'sacrifice' them as if they were so many lambs or young birds; meanwhile the mother stood by without a tear or a moan."[11]

---

[11] Dennis, 2539.

Really, that is what a civilized culture looks like? We need to be absolutely clear, civilization does not exist where Christianity and the church does not exist, and Christianity and the church (in its most biblical form) has not existed here for quite some time, and politics and elections, although a very important responsibility for every individual Christian, is not what is going to bring true civilization back to this land, or any land, for that matter.

It was early Christian culture, during Rome and its heyday, which brought and taught a sanctity of life, one of the hallmarks of true civilization.

The Didache, a first century pastoral manual stated, "thou shalt not murder a child by abortion nor kill them when born."[12]

The Letter of Barnabas also states, "you shall not abort a child nor, again, commit infanticide."[13]

It was the actions of Christians in the third century like Callistus who provided refuge to abandon children by placing them in Christian homes; and Benignus of Dijon who offered nourishment and protection to abandoned children, some who

---

[12] Ibid.
[13] Ibid.

reportedly had disabilities caused by unsuccessful abortions.[14]

The prophets of the Old Testament had a calling, and spoke of certain things in an evil age. Let us take a look at where the people of god in the Old Testament ended up and how they got there.

Then Solomon built a high place for Chemosh the abomination of Moab, and for Molech the abomination of the Ammonites, on the mountain east of Jerusalem. (1 Kings 11:7)

When the king of Moab saw that the battle was going against him, he took with him 700 swordsmen to break through, opposite the King of Edom, but they could not. [27] Then he took his oldest son who was to reign in his place and offered him for a burnt offering on the wall. And there came great wrath against Israel. And they withdrew from him and returned to their own land. (2 Kings 3:26-27)

Ahaz was twenty years old when he began to reign, and he reigned sixteen years in Jerusalem. And he did not do what was right in the eyes of the Lord his God, as his father David had done, but he walked in the way of the kings of Israel. He even burned his son as an offering, according to the despicable practices of the nations whom the Lord drove out before the people of Israel.(2 Kings 16:2-3)

---

[14] Ibid.

And this occurred because the people of Israel had sinned against the Lord their god, who had brought them up out of the land of Egypt from under the hand of pharaoh king of Egypt, and had feared other gods and walked in the customs of the nations whom the Lord drove out before the people of Israel, and in the customs that the kings of Israel had practiced. And the people of Israel did secretly against the Lord their God things that were not right. They built for themselves high places in all their towns, from watchtower to fortified city. They set up for themselves pillars and Asherim on every high hill and under every green tree, and there they made offerings on all the high places, as the nations did whom the Lord carried away before them. And they did wicked things, provoking the Lord to anger, and they served idols, of which the Lord had said to them, "you shall not do this." Yet the Lord warned Israel and Judah by every prophet and every seer, saying, "Turn from your evil ways and keep my commandments and my statutes, in accordance with all the law that I commanded your fathers, and that I sent to you by my servants the prophets."

But they would not listen, but were stubborn, as their fathers had been, who did not believe in the Lord their God. They despised his statutes and his covenant that he made with their fathers and the warnings that he gave them. They went after false idols and became false, and they followed the nations that were around them, concerning whom the Lord had commanded them that they should not do like them. And they abandoned all the commandments of the Lord their God, and made for themselves metal images of two calves; and they made an Asherah and worshiped all the host of heaven and served Baal. And they burned their sons and their daughters as offerings and used divination and omens and sold themselves to do evil in the sight of the Lord, provoking him to anger. (2 Kings 17:7-17)

I would submit that this is an evil age, and therefore we are called, just as the prophets of old, to call the people out. We are no better than the Romans. We are no longer a civilized society, as we murder the gifts of new life that God blesses us with.

I will say, in the name of our great Jehovah and his son Jesus Christ...

And you took your sons and your daughters, whom you had borne to me, and these you sacrificed to them to be devoured. Were your whorings so small a matter that you slaughtered my children and delivered them up as an offering by fire to them? (Ezekiel 16:20-21)

Therefore, the Lord was very angry with America, and he removed them out of his sight. None was left but the faithful church.

In closing today, we find ourselves right where we ended up last week. It is important to notice that this issue of abortion is a symptom, a very important symptom, but a symptom like all of the others. Every important topic that will be discussed in this presidential election cycle is a symptom. They all point to the disease, and that disease is found squarely in the hearts of each and every man. It is part of our calling, as those stars from last week, God's glory reflectors, to show each and every person the cure, even as Paul tells us in Romans 5…

Therefore, as one trespass led to condemnation for all men, so one act of righteousness leads to justification and life for all men. For as by the one man's disobedience the many were made sinners, so by the one man's obedience the many will be made righteous. (Romans 5:18-19)

So that, as sin reigned in death, grace also might reign through righteousness leading to eternal life through Jesus Christ our Lord. (Romans 5:21)

Conclusion and Charge

So, I challenge each and every one of us today, what is your mission and ministry? If we are truly worried about losing this country, then let us be those who are doing the only thing that will save it; making disciples of all the nations, baptizing them in the name of the Father and of the Son and of the Holy Spirit, and teaching them to observe all that Jesus has commanded.

In 1997 a compilation of Dr. Seuss stories was published into one book with the distinct purpose of being read to babies while they were in the womb. It was titled "Oh, Baby, the Places You'll Go."[15]

---

[15] Rabe.

May our prayer and our goal be that this can once again be said with integrity not only about the Church in this land, but about all of the children as well! Oh, baby, the places you'll go, indeed.